Quinn Collectibles Presents...

MONSTER BABES

A Creepy Glam Coloring Book

By Stephanie A. Quinn

SCRIBBLE AWAY!

Use this page to test your colors!

Betty Bandages

Age: 55 Human Years

Location: At a doctor's office near you...

She has won numerous awards for her paintings.

Carol Critters

Age: 28 Human Years

Location: Hiding in the corner of the room...

She has friends of all sizes!

Nancy Nibbles

Age: 280 Vampire Years

Location: Napping in a funeral home.

She makes all of her own jewelry.

Sarah Skull

Age: 150 Human Years

Location: The candy aisle of the supermarket.
They say "Everytime you sneeze, Sarah Skull
listens..."

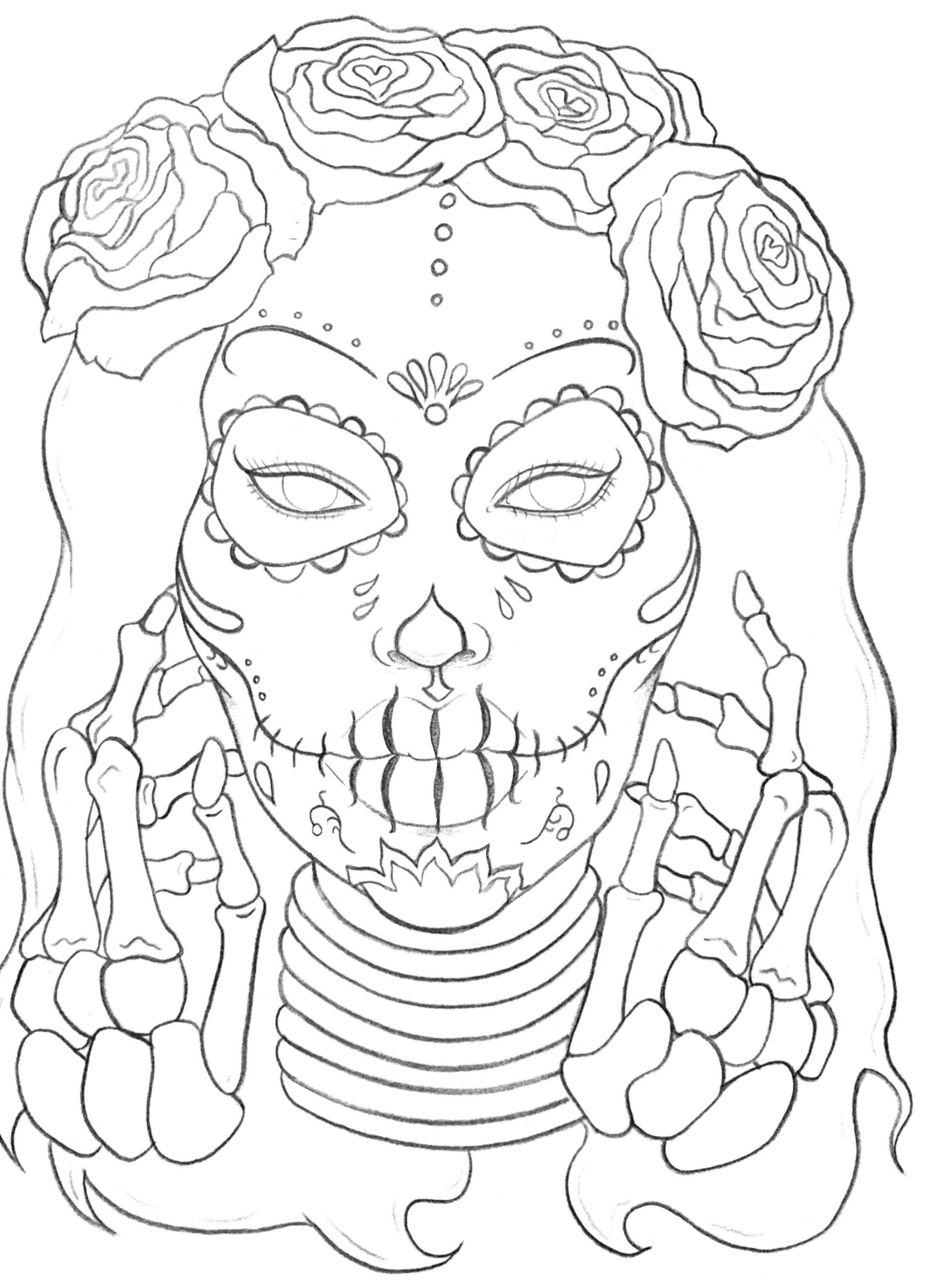

Cherry Cheetah

Age: 18 Cat Years
Location: On the prowl...
She loves cookie dough ice cream.

Gabbie Ghoul

Age: 21 Human Years, 3 Zombie years
Location: Hanging out at a graveyard near you.
She is really itchy.

Sammi Spells

Age: 23 Human Years

Location: The local Wizard Academy's hat store.

She has got more brooms than rooms!

Wendy Weeds

Age: 62 Ancient Plant Years

Location: Hiding under a flower petal in a remote field.

She has a perfect credit score!

Lily Labrador

Age: 20 Dog Years

Location: Currently chasing a car.

She loves getting dressed up!

Mel Milkyway

Age: 1533 Alien Years

Location: An Intergalactic record store.

She is a really good cook.

Dolores Doll

Age: 30 Plastic Years

Location: Asleep in a display case.

She loves scary movies.

Ronda Reaper

Age: Predates Time

Location: A subterranean cafe.

During the summer she works at the movie

theater.

Mona Motherboard

Age: 2 Weeks Old

Location: In a box at the department store.

She loves the sound of human laughter.

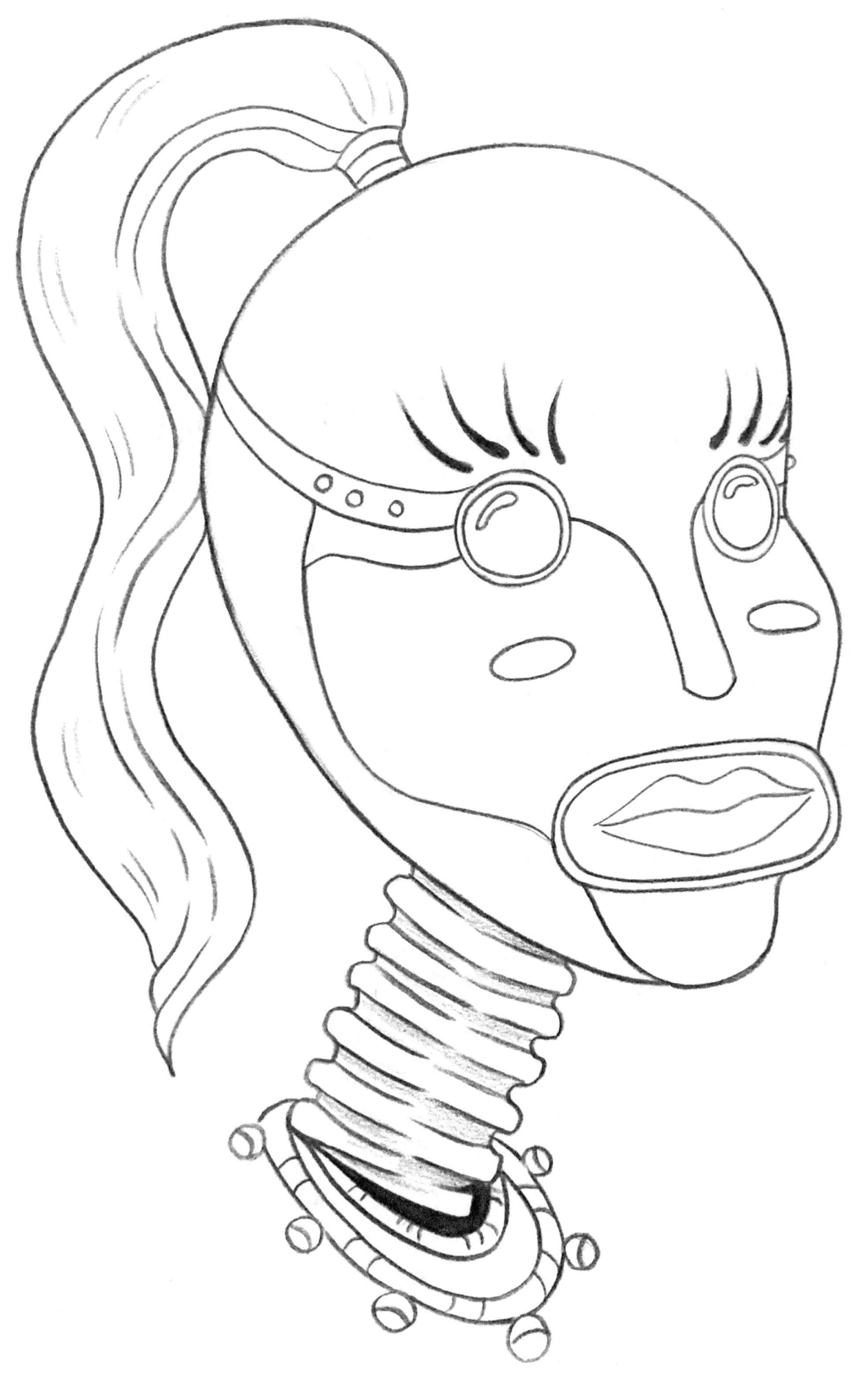

Rebecca Returned

Age: 18 Human Years, 1 Zombie Year
Location: Living at the nuclear power plant.
Nobody knows, but she glows in the dark!

Becky Boo

Age: 17 Ghost Years

Location: Haunting the local shoe store.

Don't leave her alone in the kitchen!

Whitney Winks

Age: 19 Monster Years

Location: Studying for an Eye Exam.

Her offspring is destined to rule the world.

Bolly Bony

Age: 21 Unicorn Years

Location: The forgotten Realm.

She is really good at guitar.

Kat Kandymancer

Age: 53 Sugar Years

Location: Anywhere but the Dentist's Office.

Everything about her is made of candy.

Age: 35 Human Years

Location: The Municipal Monster Hospital.

Don't ask why she's nasty...

Gertie Goldfish

Age: 40 Fish Years

Location: The middle of the Atlantic Ocean.

She just recently learned to swim!

Shelby Succubus

Age: 3500 Monster Years

Location: A secluded island...

She loves jewelry and her birthstone is an opal.

Chelsea Chomp

Age: 25 Monster Years

Location: At a grocery store near you...

She never goes a day without flossing.

India Ink

Age: 22 Human Years

Location: Currently working at the Post Office.

She loves trying new ice cream flavors.

Fingerella

Age: Unknown

Location: Safe and warm in a mitten.

She blesses those who kiss their index fingers
before going to sleep...

Melty Mary

Age: 32 Monster Years

Location: Working at the glue factory.

She loves to try new things!

Peggy Pierce

Age: 28 Human Years

Location: Interning at the local Tattoo Parlor.

Her favorite food is sushi.

Suzie Scramble

Age: 19 Monster Years

Location: Hanging out at the Monster Library.

She loves blind dates.

Clara Clown

Age: 24 Monster Years

Location: A birthday party.

She takes her job very seriously.

Fiona Fly

Age: 16 Insect Years

Location: Inspecting food at the local market.

She always keeps her promises.

Nora Nails

Age: 26 Monster Years

Location: The International Monster Airport.

She is currently working as the first ever monster flight attendant.

Quinn Collectibles
Coloring Books!
By Stephanie A. Quinn

Art For Everyone!

Here at Quinn Collectibles, we believe in Art For Everyone!

No Pressure - You don't have to be Michelangelo to enjoy a relaxing session of coloring. Now is the time to let your imagination run wild and put some blue lipstick on that golden retriever!

Experimentation - Finished coloring your page and notice that you have some space leftover? Why not draw a flower of your own and color it in!

Fun - If you're not having fun, what are you doing? Life is short, grab a box of your favorite crayons and get funky!